HOW I THINK ABOUT HOW MEN THINK

All Women Don't Think Alike

Reader's Discretion Advised

Copyright 2022 by Michele Rosales

All rights reserved. No part of this book may be reproduced or utilized in any form or by any means, electronic or mechanical, including photocopying and recording, or by an information storage and retrieval system, without written permission from the author.

Men assume all women think alike. However, all women don't think alike. Enter the mind of a woman who has a different perspective of men…uncensored!

ISBN: 978-0-578-38355-2

Printed in the United States of America

HERE COMES THE JUDGE

A husband and wife were in court and the husband complained to a judge that his wife won't have sex with him when he wants to get his rocks off. She said she doesn't always feel like it. The judge said that's her body and she has a right to her body and a right to say no.

I'm not sure what's wrong with women. Technically sex was designed for marriage. No matter how you spin it, sex was designed for marriage. Therefore, the husband was right. When you are married, your body belongs to your husband. Even better, your husband's dick belongs to you.

What's wrong with women. This is my body they say. But when you are married, it's your husband's body as well. Check. Checkmate.

THE BIG LIE

All men cheat. All men don't cheat. Just because your mate cheated and most men you meet cheat doesn't mean every man in the United States and in the whole world cheat. The other big lie – all men have a high sex drive and need sex so much that they have to have it every night and just can't resist a woman. They act like women don't have high sex drives so they make you believe it's only men.

But aren't they having sex with women? If your sex drive was that high, you would find yourself a wife then you would have it available all the time. I know, it's available all the time without a wife. And you ain't getting it all the time. You just make women think you are. When you reach 40, we know better. Oh but what if the chemistry is not there with your wife, you say.

CHEMISTRY

What is chemistry between two people? Men look for wives with their dicks. Whatever happened to if I love you, I know I will enjoy you. But no. Men and some women gotta test the package first.

Can someone please explain. Chemistry is a class I took. Has anyone else actually taken Chemistry? You have General Chemistry, Organic Chemistry, Inorganic Chemistry. What does atoms, protons and neutrons have to do with love? You take two hydrogens and one oxygen and you have H2O aka water. Add an Oxygen to that and you have peroxide. Starting to fizzle up a bit. So you have some carbon with a double strand to oxygen then a single strand to hydrogen which leads to drugs being made. Keep on building those chemical reactions and you have an explosion. It's called gonorrhea.

There's some new shit out now…chlamydia. You mean there are some new additional symptoms? Not covered by gonorrhea, syphilis, HIV, warts, Herpes. What d.. Gotta keep making sure there's chemistry between two people. You gotta keep on putting your dick in all that different pussy…condoms. That won't help anymore. There's gonna be some new shit that will burn right through that condom and burn your dick up.

I hate it when a man want to be devoted because he doesn't want his dick to burn. What about love being the reason?

Otherwise, he'll go cheat with a virgin...just to be sure.

MESSAGE TO YOUNG MEN

Most men love hoes so most men can be hoes. But they have an excuse… I'm a man. That's how we roll. It's in our DNA they say. They think they're impressive. All older woman are not impressed with you wanting to put your dicks in us. We are not looking for boy toys… just a dick that works. Not sure why married older women so concerned about her husband going through a mid-life crisis. Let him go find a younger woman. That will free up the younger men. But not too young.

Young men need to find yourselves a wife and be committed so that when you are in your 50s, you will have a wife to pray for your limp dick. Otherwise you will have to come see me or women like me when you in your 50s. Perhaps if you didn't sling it so much with different women when you were young, you can do more than eat pussy. However, I can help you with your problem.

BEHIND YOUR BACK

So now you're in your 50s with a broke dick. You come to me because you know I will fix your dick. Come on in my room and look at this nice 3 inch needle I'm going to stick in your ass. Just like your wife, fiancé, girlfriend had to trust yo cheating ass behind her back, you have to trust me behind your back with this big ass needle full of testosterone. And I will let you see it first. Now drop your drawers and bend over. I will take that needle and jab it in your ass and you will let me..now keep still while it's in your ass. If you move it may hit your sciatic nerve and you might not walk good. But first I have to aspirate and make sure I didn't hit a blood vessel. Gotta see if blood is in the testosterone liquid I'm getting ready to shove in your funky ass. I don't see blood so now I can push it in. Now I can take the 3 inch big bore needle out your ass. Oops I think you need a bandaid. Make sure you sign out at the front desk when you leave. See you in two weeks for the next 20 years…broke ass dick. Yes you can have a sample of Viagra too for the weekend. No, I do not want to date your broke dick ass.

OWNERSHIP

I own a house and a timeshare. The only other thing I need to own is a dick. You don't own a dick if you not married. You don't own a dick if you married to a liar and a cheater. Most men don't want you to own their dicks. They just want to own your pussy.

TITLES

You see men choose a woman he wants to put his dick in the most. Perhaps she can cook and is really pretty. But he want to still look around using his dick so he gives her a title to keep her happy. It's called girlfriend. You really don't own the dick, you are borrowing it. He just wants you to think it's yours.

Then he finds a woman who he wants to put his dick in because "he's a man."

To keep his woman happy he gives her a new title...fiancé. Plus it comes with a rock. I think men designed the wedding set. Notice the engagement ring is bigger and more expensive. It will keep you occupied showing your family and friends what a big rock you have while he puts his dick somewhere else because she came after him like he wanted. Men know how to say no and push other women away. But they want to play games. So they buy an expensive $5,000 maybe $10,000 engagement ring. Make you stay engaged and not own his dick even longer. The wedding band sure is smaller. How nicely well thought of… make her think she owns the dick.

Buy me an engagement ring…a big ole expensive rock. I will go show my family and friends. We will chip away. Then you will want it back. And I will tell you we smoked it. It was a diamond after all. We didn't feel anything. You're out of thousands of dollars and I'm scarred because I wanted to marry your sorry ass. Not because we didn't make it…don't be conceited. But because I was dumb enough to look at you in the first place. I'll be glad you gone. Oh the other trick, threaten to leave her after the two of you are established. Make her squirm. She'll forgive you when you cheat. Why? You gave her a title.

MESSAGE TO CELEBRITY MEN

There is a myth. But this is the truth. Every woman does not want your big dick, rich and famous ass. A photo and autograph will suffice. If I eliminate one of those descriptions, every woman does not want your rich and famous ass. Every woman does not want your big dick rich ass. Eliminate 2 words. Every woman does not want your big dick. Every woman does not want your rich ass. Every woman does not want your famous broke ass.

Women, close your legs a few years then you don't need a big dick conceited dick slinging man who likes to accommodate every woman who comes his way. It may be easier to notice a trustworthy man and not be concerned about size.

My pussy tight so a trustworthy husband with a little dick will fit just fine. And it will stretch like it's designed to do if my trustworthy husband has a big dick.

Men, size does not matter to all of us. Money does not matter to all of us. Take your yacht, drive it out to the middle of the ocean and go fishing for some sharks. With your high position CMO CEO CCO COO PTO entrepreneur conceited ass.

STEVE HARVEY

What is wrong with Steve Harvey? Is he serious! He said never tell a man on the first date you looking for marriage. Well why not! So that cute, high sidity dick slinger will like me and want another date with me? I'm the bitch who can cook. I may not want to serve his conceited CMO ass in the bed. Is he looking for a wife or a long term piece? So I gotta think he's so great I can't be honest and say what's on my mind? Just because a woman mentions marriage doesn't mean she has chosen you to marry. She is determining if she wants a second date with your cute dumb ass. You may not be worth it. Then I can advise you to go try sky diving or mountain climbing. Go on Steve's yacht.

CELEBRITY PUSSY

Why would a man destroy his whole family just for some celebrity pussy? If you put a bag over your head so you couldn't see who it was, would you really know the difference? Does your sperm change colors? Yellow sperm plus green sperm equals flames…chemistry. I bet y'all have invested in fire extinquishers

MESSAGE TO MARRIED MEN

Stop flirting. It's not manly nor attractive. No serious-minded woman will want you except the woman you fooled into marrying your "think you got it like that" attitude. If your wife can't trust you behind her back, then I can't trust you behind mine…especially if you're a hair stylist. Why not keep your cheating, flirty, funky dick ass single. Your buddies can trust you, right? Stupid soup eatin' ass.

THE REAL REASON MOST MEN CHEAT

I finally realize the real reason most men cheat. They're weak. Weak head of households. The weakest ones are proud to buy the magnum jumbo condoms. They say, "I'm a player." That's right little boy. You play in a man's body. You are weak with no inner strength. You don't have to cheat. Just tell us you want someone else and get a divorce and leave. All women won't be ruined for life because you decided you wanted to move on. We won't be mad. We're actually looking for a reason to divorce your sorry ass. We just didn't let you know it.

I know some women say oh no. I have been with him for 20 years and he's worth fighting for, the marriage is worth fighting for….wah wah wah wah. Duh..don't you have 20 plus more years left to be with a real man? Boy bye!

ALL WOMEN DON'T THINK ALIKE

There are not 10 women to one man. It only appears that way when he marries into your family and surrounded by all your female family and friends and wants to put his dick in all of them. That's how they make women feel desperate…a male shortage. Most men want women to believe anything other than da truth…sex was designed for marriage.

SeniorFitChic

www.ingramcontent.com/pod-product-compliance
Lightning Source LLC
Chambersburg PA
CBRC091958300426
44109CB00007BA/161